JOURNEY TO FREEDOM
Study Guide Series

JOURNEY

TO HEALTHY LIVING

Freedom from Body Image & Food Issues

YMCA OF MIDDLE TENNESSEE
SCOTT REALL

THOMAS NELSON
Since 1798

NASHVILLE   DALLAS   MEXICO CITY   RIO DE JANEIRO   BEIJING

Published in Nashville, Tennessee, by Thomas Nelson. Thomas Nelson is a registered trademark of Thomas Nelson, Inc.

Thomas Nelson, Inc., titles may be purchased in bulk for educational, business, fund-raising, or sales promotional use. For information, please e-mail SpecialMarkets@ThomasNelson.com.

Scripture quotations marked NKJV are from THE NEW KING JAMES VERSION. © 1982 by Thomas Nelson, Inc. Used by permission. All rights reserved.

Scripture quotations marked NIV are from HOLY BIBLE: NEW INTERNATIONAL VERSION®. ©1973, 1978, 1984 by International Bible Society. Used by permission of Zondervan Publishing House. All rights reserved.

Scripture quotations marked NCV are from New Century Version®. © 2005 by Thomas Nelson, Inc. Used by permission. All rights reserved.

Scripture quotations marked KJV are from KING JAMES VERSION.

To find a YMCA near you, please visit the following Web sites:

United States of America: www.ymca.com
Canada: www.ymca.ca
England: www.ymca.org.uk
Australia: www.ymca.org.au

Visit www.restoreymca.org for more information on Restore, a life-changing ministry of the YMCA.

ISBN 978-1-4185-0769-5

Printed in the United States of America.
08 09 10 11 RRD 5 4 3 2 1

CONTENTS

I n my twenty years at the YMCA, I have witnessed a revolution in the area of body image. Everybody is concerned about the way they look, which is normal. But I've seen that too much of a good thing easily becomes an obsession.

Perhaps you have selected this book because you want to change some aspect of your body. I encourage you to become not a perfect specimen of the human race, but the person *you* desire to be. This should be our goal in this study. So what does having a healthy body image look like? When a person has a healthy body weight and is physically fit, but is obsessed with food and with working out, or secretly exhibits signs of bulimia or anorexia, this is not healthy. Eventually these behaviors tear the body down and create addictions and all sorts of emotional problems.

For years, when I struggled with depression and low self-esteem, I tried to control those struggles by focusing on how I looked. Since I felt unacceptable, I thought if I could present myself as physically acceptable to the world, then somehow I could mask my deep sense of inadequacy. I desired affirmation from people and achieved it. I was good at deceiving people, to my own detriment. Most thought I was healthy when, in fact, I was sick. My self-esteem depended on how people viewed my physical image.

Watch the ads on TV for exercise programs and diets and you'll discover our nation's obsession with body image. We've witnessed this at Restore Ministries. There's a polarization with body image—extremes in opposite directions. One direction leads to obsessions with exercise and food. We want to feel accepted and loved through acceptance of our bodies. The other direction leads to addictions with food. We use food to help us deal with the pain and discomfort of not having a perfect body. We give up on obtaining the perfect body and establish a sick relationship with food. Food becomes a way to comfort the pain of feeling flawed.

What are the truths regarding our relationship with our bodies and with food? Throughout this study, we'll identify patterns that are not healthy and take steps to move toward healthy patterns. Our goal is to make peace with our bodies and with our lives. Obesity is at an all-time high in our country. Eating disorders are more prevalent than they've ever been. Food and body obsessions are destroying the quality of our lives, and we need to find a path to freedom. Today I don't have the near-perfect physical body that I had ten years ago—but I am far healthier than I have ever been. I am comfortable with how I look, I love to be active and eat well because of how it makes me feel (instead of how it makes me look), and my self-esteem and self-worth are not derived from how I look. At the same time, I am aware that at times I still feed something in me that's not hunger.

My desire, as you read through this study, is for you to identify your eating and exercising habits. What are your patterns with food and exercise? Are they obsessive? Are they normal? How well are you doing with body image? Let's discover a way to make fitness and health not an obsession, but something that adds years and enjoyment to our lives.

CHAPTER ONE

THE OBSESSION

A fashion photographer once fired Carol Alt, former *Sports Illustrated* cover girl, after he spent a day on location trying to hide her extra ounces of flesh behind rocks. He said her body was "too jiggly" for her bikini.[1] Imagine that—a well-known supermodel fired over her seemingly imperfect body! This is a sad commentary on our beauty-crazed society, and it's not just women who are under the microscope. There's been a change over the last decade in how males view their bodies, too. According to a study by the research firm American Sports Data, the "number of men exercising has soared—8.5 million men now have health club memberships. . . . And men spend an average of 90.8 days a year in the club (that's over 2,000 hours). That's nine days a year more than women."[2]

We live in a culture that is obsessed with body image, and it's killing us—for some, literally, and for others it's killing our enjoyment of life. We deal with a variety of struggles at Restore Ministries, and we've seen that one of the deadliest struggles is obsession with body image. We will go to extremes to look beautiful and are never quite satisfied with what we see in the mirror. This obsession kills the will to live freely, and we willingly put ourselves in bondage to it. The problem is rampant. I honestly don't know if I have ever met a woman who hasn't at one time or another uttered those two awful words: "I'm fat."

The advent of media and movies hasn't helped. Our environments are flooded with imagery that contributes to illogical thoughts about what is a healthy body image and how it can be obtained. Looking back offers insight into how our obsession with body image has evolved over the last fifty or so years. When I view classic movies from the last fifty years, I see an evolution of body image, especially in women. What was attractive fifty years ago would be considered obese today. It's ridiculous, really. The "perfect female body" has been a million different things at a million different times. Fifteenth-century Renaissance artists portrayed perfection as it was seen then—when women were full figured. But times changed and more and more women desired a trim waistline, and thus the corset was born.

In the 1920s, thin lips, mannish chins, and flat breasts were suddenly all the rage. In the thirties, women were wearing short hair and penciled-in eyebrows, and their curves were in all the places women hate to have curves today. The forties saw lean women as fashionable, but the movie star beauties still had a certain amount of curve to them. In the fifties women were curvier still—you've seen the then-current "perfection" of Marilyn Monroe. By our standards she would have been considered a heavy woman; she wore a size 16 dress at one point. But even "perfect" Marilyn struggled with her weight and the public's perception of her body image.

This body image standard continued to shift wildly throughout the sixties and seventies, followed by the big-hair eighties and short-hair nineties. In all of these periods, the "ideal figure" shifted and transformed. Today, most of those earlier figures wouldn't be considered desirable or even acceptable. But trends in style, size, and shape will continue to change as long as we keep tuning in and reading the magazines. The cycle will continue.

This image of physical perfection, this ideal figure, is being nicely packaged and labeled as *attractive*. It's being sold to us as a product, as something that will bring love and fulfillment. These reasons alone can create obsessions and an unhealthy lifestyle. Most of us will never be able to attain this ideal physical body. And those who can, usually do so because they're working out an absurd number of hours, hiring personal trainers, and severely restricting their food intakes. There are numerous contributing factors to how we look, and we have no control over many of those things—they're genetic! And genetics can ultimately have a huge effect on the way our bodies react to diets or workout routines. So if what we're obsessed with is perfection, we're in for years of utter frustration if we can't make peace with our genes. Many popular singers today have absurdly firm, small bodies, and are no comparison to the singers of the forties, fifties, and sixties. And these are our role models, are they not? Movie stars are another standard "ideal." How can an entire generation of women expect to look like Julia Roberts, Sharon Stone, or Demi Moore? And the next generation is already aspiring to look like Kiera Knightley, Jessica Alba, and the Olsen twins. Models are another issue. Their body standards have been an unachievable ideal for decades—but even in the last twenty years, they've gone from being tall and curvy to tall and emaciated.

If you look at the fashions today, you begin to understand the role that perfection and sexuality play in our day-to-day existence. The cheerleading outfits today could pass for bathing suits, women's shorts could pass for underwear, and a perfect, hard, "sexy" body is the only acceptable frame for a lot of the popular styles. Fifty years ago, the more clothing a woman wore and the more curves she had was what made her beautiful and desirable. Now, what used to be considered beautiful is unacceptable, even grotesque. Where does the madness end? What will we be wearing in the next twenty years? It's a scary thought, and the consequences could be absolutely devastating.

Tilly's Story

As a little girl, I loved the idea of romance. I would dream of living in a far-off land with my prince, wearing beautiful dresses and loving my life. I imagined myself as the delicate heroine at the end of all the fairytale stories until one fateful day when I was old enough to understand that I was not as perfect as the fairytale princesses in my books. I can remember, as a very young girl, looking in the mirror while standing next to my older and younger sister and realizing I was taller and chubbier than both of them. My dreams and images of what I should look like were quickly shattered in that mirror. At an early age, I became obsessed with my body and the way that I looked—not only the way others saw me, but the way I saw myself.

Then I began ballet class at the age of nine. Now my dreams were of being a ballerina. But standing in front of those mirrors, glaring at the slender girls around me, I quickly realized that I was not built like them. I was not as graceful either. I would leave class feeling inadequate and terrible about myself. I became obsessed with mirrors. Every time that I would walk past one, I would stop and look just to see if anything had changed. To see if I had suddenly become thin like everyone else. To judge how content I was with my body. I was obsessed. I couldn't focus on anything else but what I looked like or what I weighed.

Studies have shown that 80 percent of women are unhappy with their body image.[3] That's eight out of ten! What are women willing to go through in order to obtain this perfection? This problem seems to be creating extremes. Some continue to eat and eat, and others restrict and restrict. But most of us live in a constant struggle with weight fluctuations—being neither obese nor extremely thin—and never quite attaining the ideal body we strive for. Men do not often hold themselves to these sorts of visual standards, but they have their own unachievable aspirations. The ideals for men in our culture are people like Arnold

Schwarzenegger, Sylvester Stallone, or Brad Pitt. These men are unbelievably buff and ridiculously tough. The media glorifies them in such a way that the average man is left to conclude that this is what makes you a man.

A new addiction has been added to a list of common ones in the last decade: plastic surgery. Both men and women return again and again for nips and tucks in their quest for perfection. A woman named Cindy Jackson is considered a plastic surgery legend. In the eighties she decided to go where none had gone before—completely changing her appearance from "plain" to "perfect." She underwent forty-seven procedures in nine separate surgeries. She has had one full face-lift; three "mini" face-lifts (one lower, two upper); three eyelid surgeries (one upper, two lower); one upper lip lift; liposuction on her knees, thighs, abdomen, waist, and jawline; two nose operations; breast augmentation; breast implant removal; cheek implants; bottom lip implant; chin reduction; hair transplantation to cover face-lift scars; two partial dermabrasions; two chemical peels; two laser resurfacings; facial thread vein removal; mole removal; scar revision; semi-permanent and permanent make-up; numerous temporary filler injections; cosmetic dentistry; and laser tooth whitening. She has been called the "human Barbie," and has inspired many to follow suit in pursuit of the perfection she believes she has found. It has only been in the last couple of decades that technology has made plastic surgery addiction possible, but in society's limitless pursuit of perfection, it hasn't taken long for this addiction to catch on.

It is impossible to understand the impact of botched or overdone procedures without seeing the images—a quick search online can produce dozens of photos of less-than-perfect faces and figures. When you look at some of these images, you experience an undeniable visual jolt. Worse still is the deep sense of sadness you feel when you understand the cycle these people are stuck in—the dissatisfaction and relentlessness of the standards they are setting themselves up against.

Obsession with body image as it relates to eating disorders and obesity is simply another symptom of the same problem. Various studies offer shocking figures regarding both underweight and overweight people in our country. Even as recently as 1991, none of the fifty American states had obesity prevalence rates over 20 percent. In 2005, only four states were *under* 20 percent, while seventeen states had prevalence rates equal to or greater than 25 percent, and three of those states (Louisiana, Mississippi, and West Virginia) had prevalence equal to or greater than 30 percent.[4] These are only the obese; these people are included in the sixty or so percent of the American population that is overweight.

There is a discrepancy in the numbers because so many cases go unreported, but somewhere between 5 and 15 percent of women and around one million men are anorexic. Around 20 to 25 percent have some sort of eating disorder—although again, these numbers are difficult to estimate, considering the shame and secrecy that accompanies these struggles. Certainly a majority of those suffering are young women. Some have estimated that around 90 percent are females between the ages of fifteen and twenty-five, and 11 percent of high school girls, have been diagnosed with eating disorders.[5] However, these are disorders without boundaries. Men, older women, and children younger than fifteen have all been shown to be susceptible. "Bigorexia" is now a common term referring to men who push themselves to become more and more muscular, obsessing dangerously the way an anorexic pushes to become thinner.

As a young man, I struggled with body image. I felt that the one thing in my life I could control was my body. Mentally and spiritually, I was a wreck. At the time, I didn't understand how my obsession with body image would eventually play into my addictions. I started lifting weights in seventh or eighth grade in my basement. I kept going through high school and college and throughout my whole adult life, perhaps more intensely as an adult. A deep sense of insecurity provided the drive to do this. I felt that if I could physically look as perfect as possible, it would give me some sense of control over my insecurities. Yet nothing had changed on the inside. I still thought, despite anyone's affirmation about my body image, that I was unacceptable. I saw the scars on my face, the tiny bald spot that was growing, and my insecurity was an uncontrollable obsession. I thought I could control people's opinions of me by having the perfect body. But on the inside I was just as lost, lonely, and insecure as I had ever been. My ability to experience intimacy was gone. I was a fearful young man who didn't have anything to offer. My cup was empty—I had a hole in my soul—and I was keeping all this in a perfect physical body. Once I got into a relationship, I had nothing more to give.

When I was a child, food became a comfort to me. On special nights before watching a movie on television, we'd go to the market and get some soda, a bag of chips, and a carton of ice cream—then we'd sit down and eat all of it. We'd go to bed with a full stomach and a sense of well-being and comfort. I realize that I still associate food with comfort.

Low-fat food was unheard of back then. Now we have all these diet foods, and obesity is higher than it's ever been. It seems no one is active for enjoyment's sake. When I was kid, there were three television channels and nothing on during the day. And there was no air-conditioning. Now you have three or four hundred channels on cable, and families have a TV in every room. And computers—there were no computers back then. No Internet. No e-mail. And we were probably healthier because of it. I was born into an active, athletic family with parents who kicked us out of the house in the afternoons because there was nothing to do inside. We were playing, walking, and riding bikes all day, every day. I learned the incredible enjoyment of being active. We weren't "working out;" we were playing. Today I find walking enjoyable. I go for two or three walks a day sometimes and I love seeing families out walking together.

BEGINNING YOUR JOURNEY

We only have one opportunity at life. If we abuse our bodies, we will be on the path to bad health or early death. God made our bodies to carry our spirits around for our human experience. That's it. Our bodies are decaying, but our souls are maturing. "Human life is like grass; we grow like a flower in the field. After the wind blows, the flower is gone, and there is no sign of where it was" (Ps. 103:15–16 NCV). If this is the fate of humans, then we must look for something eternal. Our bodies aren't timeless; they are withering. I'm not saying you should give up, stop working out, and stop eating right. I'm only saying that we should give our souls—the part of us that is eternal—equal attention as we do our bodies. If I'm obsessing about my body—about what I eat—I can't possibly be concerned about my soul or the souls of others. If I'm obsessing, I'm all about myself and nothing else.

It seems like the US leads the world in external obsession—we have all these disillusioned people who unfortunately believe that a perfect body will make them happy. Paul Laurence Dunbar's poem, "Sympathy," speaks to this problem:

> *I know why the caged bird sings, ah me,*
> *When his wing is bruised and his bosom sore,—*
> *When he beats his bars and he would be free;*
> *It's not a carol of joy or glee,*
> *But a prayer that he sends from his heart's deep core,*
> *But a plea, that upward to Heaven he flings—*
> *I know why the caged bird sings."*[6]

We are a society of caged birds. We live in the bondage of our self-made cages. Some of us have unwittingly caged our spirits. Our hearts long to be free, and yet we continue to beat our wings and our hearts against our self-made prison bars of perfection.

We can't claim ignorance any longer; we know what we're doing. I know when I reach for addiction that it is going to break my heart. And yet I keep doing it. I believe that I don't have the power to stop, and this is the power an addiction has over us. People ask me about my struggle with addiction, "Why do you do it?" And I say, "I don't know why." Paul says this is in the New Testament: "The thing I know to be wrong I do."[7]

The caged bird only wants to sing—to be fully alive. And we "live lives inferior to ourselves," not alive. We want to escape, to feel alive, so we turn to food or some other addiction. By the time we discover it can't fulfill or comfort us, we can't stop returning to it. So we stay trapped in our self-made cages and continue to beat our wings. There's only one answer: the healing power of Jesus Christ. He sets us free and gives us life as we've never known. Psalm 124:7 says, "We have escaped like a bird out of the fowler's snare; the snare has been broken, and we have escaped" (NIV).

If we accept what we cannot change—as the serenity prayer says— then what can we change? Should we change? For health, perhaps. If we're harming our hearts, limiting our mobility, and shortening our lives, our behavior will limit us in fulfilling our potential as one of God's children. It will impact us spiritually and emotionally, because God made us spirit, mind, and body. But our significance should lie in one person, the person of Christ.

Does God want me to continue to be sedentary, wasting my health away? Absolutely not! Does he want me to be obsessed with food and my body to the point that it's destroying me? Absolutely not! God wants me to have a healthy relationship with self and food, to balance. And that's what we will continue to explore in this book.

Some of us need motivation to become active and enjoy life. We need to find people who will encourage us. We need to change destructive habits. Some of us need to be free from an eating disorder, from obsession, or from an unhealthy sedentary lifestyle. All of us need to be set free by the power of the Holy Spirit. No one can do it alone. We need to strive for a healthy balance, for a relationship with our bodies as God intended it to be. We all need to know that God loves us—no matter what we do or look like.

There are people in this world who are stupid enough to tell us we are ugly. You may have looked in the mirror or stood on the scale and decided that you're ugly or unacceptable. You might have had horrible things said to you. But there is something you must understand: You are loved as you are. Every curve. Every surface—inside and out. Every flaw. I won't say you don't have flaws; you're human, and that's what we humans are about. But your flaws, both of character and of person, are loved as part of who you are. You've experienced things that have led you to where you are today. But you are loved—by a God who knows every nook and cranny of who you are. So let's begin the journey to healthy self-awareness.

REFLECTION QUESTIONS

What is your relationship with food? Give specific examples of your behavior toward food.

How long has it been this way?

Can you remember a time, as a child or adult, when your relationship with food was different?

How is your relationship with your body?

a. What do you think about your body?

b. What are the things you dislike about your body?

c. What are the things you love about it?

d. What have you actively or obsessively tried to change about your body?

Think of someone in your life who you love unconditionally. What prevents you from loving and accepting yourself in the same manner?

Based on your answers above, what internal messages are you sending yourself about your value?

REFLECTIONS

REFLECTIONS

REFLECTIONS

CHAPTER TWO

TELLING OURSELVES LIES

WHAT DO YOU SEE IN THE MIRROR?

I've never met a woman who was totally pleased with her body. Nearly every woman I know is obsessed with her weight. I have seen so many women standing in front of mirrors, turning and smoothing out every wrinkle and detail in order to make themselves presentable to the world. They beg and plead with the mirror to show them someone other than who they are. They secretly hope the image staring back at them will suddenly be ten pounds lighter and better looking.

But the reality is the same for all of us when we look in the mirror. We see something different to what everyone else sees. We see someone staring back at us that, frankly, we don't like very much. The image is either too fat, too ugly, not fit enough, has too many wrinkles, or is just plain ordinary. The person in the mirror is hard to love.

My wife, for example, looks in the mirror and always comments on how fat she is. I constantly tell her that she's not. She's forty-one years old and looks great. But what she sees and what I see are two different things. I've found that if she believes she's fat, that's how she sees herself.

This is her reality, her perception. I believe that 99.99 percent of people on this planet would consider her beautiful, but she is dissatisfied with the way she looks. When I see her obsess about food, it hurts me to watch it control the quality of her life. It steals her joy. She gives energy to it, worrying about how she looks and what she eats. She even worries that how she looks could change the way I feel about her. When I tell her she looks good, she doesn't believe it.

For some reason we each have a distorted view of ourselves. We have convinced ourselves that these lies that we tell ourselves about who we are and what we are worth, are true. They have etched their way through us and infiltrated our belief systems. There is nothing that anyone can say or do to make us think differently about what we have become. These are what I like to call the "lies of our mind."

THE LIES WE BELIEVE

One of the most ridiculous lies that women tend to believe is that *they are unlovable because of what they weigh.*

Things happen to us in our lifetime—things that we have no control over—that can impact our body weight. Age, genetics, illness, accidents, mobility, and a million other factors contribute. If someone were to stop caring about you because of your weight, that would be a reflection of their shallowness. People who love us and truly care don't stop loving because of some physical change in us. True love runs much deeper than that. I know that's a difficult concept to grasp at this point—you've being hearing otherwise for so long.

Another lie that engrains itself into our minds—especially if we've been overweight for some time—is the idea that *we'll never be able to change,* that we've always been fat and always will be. That statement is a form of denial, which will basically enable us to continue in our destructive patterns. Here's the truth: anyone can change. Anyone can lose weight, and anyone can gain weight. Sure, our weight is affected by many factors, such as genetics and the like. But to deny responsibility and offer up all the reasons we're going to fail is a sure way to make that happen. In the book, *Changing for Good*, Dr. James Prochaska points out that we should not *try to change* but we should *train to change.*[1] You accomplish goals by putting small steps into practice on a daily basis. You don't run a marathon the first day you lace up your track shoes. You may need to start with a walk around the block. Then work up to jogging a mile. Then five miles. And so on. That's training. There are some people who need a change—to be more active, to be free from an addiction to food—and this is done by training to change. Daily, small differences.

I once saw an advertisement for a gym, and it featured a large picture of a ridiculously sculpted woman in a bikini—a classic example of how many fitness places advertise. This has nothing to do with fitness! It is completely cosmetic. Cosmetics and fitness are very different things. When people are training, doing positive things on a daily basis for themselves, one of the normal byproducts is losing weight. They also sleep better, feel better, and have a healthier cardiovascular system. The quality of anyone's life will improve when they are active.

One of the lies related to *I'll never change* is *I'm not normal.* An overweight person is tempted to believe they have some mechanism inside that keeps them from achieving what they see as "normal." Sadly, 60 percent of Americans are overweight. Being heavy has become very normal in this country. You're not alone in bondage—but this doesn't mean you need to stay there.

Another lie is *I will never change or be different.* This is a blatant lie. All of us have the power to change. We can add activity to our lives. We can end food addictions. We can find people who will support us. We must believe it if we are to begin to change. The most difficult part of change is getting started, and the defeating thought that we can't truly change keeps people frozen.

With God, all things are possible.[2] Some addicts believe they can never change. Yet the power to change actually comes from being powerless and having a reliance on the awesome power of God. Because it's true: *you can't* change. Left to your own power, you can do nothing. But with the right goals, the right team of supporters, you can change with the power of our God.

The most powerful, life-transforming gift we receive from God when we take the journey of recovery to a positive self-worth is true acceptance of self. If there's one thing a human being cannot function without, it's a sense of self-acceptance. If we reject ourselves, life has little to offer. If I reject my whole self because of my body, I also reject my mind and spirit. This rejection will either drive me to eat more, or drive me to restrict more. With either struggle, the first antidote is acceptance of self. My self worth and value is not determined by my body.

Tilly's Story

Each time I looked in the mirror, I saw something that I did not like, and it forced me to become adamant about perfection in a few areas of my life. By the age of twelve I had shot up in height and my body was definitely changing. I was determined not to be fat. I believed that fat girls did not live happy lives. So if I did not want to become fat, then I thought the only way to become skinny was to eat practically nothing and work out all the time. I heard that the YMCA had spin classes at 6:00 a.m. in the mornings, so I started dragging my older sister with me to class. I was pretty fit at this point. I did this for a year or two and enjoyed the results. My parents were also always on some sort of diet and dragged us along for the ride. It didn't bother me much, though, because I wanted to be thin. Eating egg whites and healthy eating only added to my pleasure.

Soon I started experimenting with how few calories I could consume, sometimes eating as few as five hundred a day. I never kept up with any particular diet for very long, but was always trying different ones for better and quicker results. It was a game. I never realized that I was telling myself a lie: that I needed to restrict my food intake to be happy. Of course, I didn't realize it was a lie at this point; I just knew that I wanted to be adored. I wanted someone to love me. I wanted to be noticed. A few people said that I should look into modeling. But what I wanted more than anything else was to be seen as beautiful, to be pursued by a boy, and to feel comfortable around people.

WHERE DO THESE LIES COME FROM?

One of the main reasons we determine our worth by body image is fear of rejection. Our assumptions about body image control the way we think about ourselves. I recently watched an episode of a reality show where girls auditioned to become Dallas Cowboy cheerleaders. Any of these women who had even a little bit of body fat would be told—in front of cameras that would broadcast to a national television audience—that they were unacceptably fat. Most of these women were amazingly attractive, and yet they were held to a ridiculous standard of perfection.

It's human nature to be wounded to the core when we're told we are not good enough in any area. We take it personally when someone says we are fat, and we allow it to dictate our acceptability. In response, some people eat to medicate those feelings of rejection, of being unacceptable. Others obsess and starve and workout and purge, trying to control the feeling of being not quite perfect.

Fear of rejection is a close cousin to the fear of abandonment. There are people who have experienced abandonment and rejection because of their imperfect bodies, and it has caused them crushing, deep pain beyond description. But here's a fact: you could look *perfect* and still be abandoned and rejected. If somebody abandons us or rejects us because of our body image, we must examine ourselves to understand why we have given the power of influence in our lives to such a critical person. Why do we feel pain when rejected by this person? Is it possible that this rejection was due to someone else's ridiculously high standards? (A perfect example is the reality show I mentioned earlier.) The love that 1 Corinthians discusses isn't superficial: "Love suffers long *and* is kind; love does not envy; love does not parade itself, is not puffed up; does not behave rudely, does not seek its own ... thinks no evil; ... rejoices in the truth; bears all things, believes all things, hopes all things.... Love never fails" (13:4–8 NKJV).

I've had many discussions around this question: Does God want you to be physically attracted to your mate? Many Christians argue that attraction in a marriage shouldn't matter. But I believe God wants us to be physically attracted to our partners. Yet physical attraction has nothing to do with love. And the more you love a person, the more attractive they become in your eyes.

Social insecurity is a fear that often plagues those with food issues and addictions, because of the isolation factor and the related fear of rejection. When we are insecure, we limit our contact with others and take fewer risks socially because of our fears. This fosters loneliness and isolation, which leads some to eat, purge, or restrict. This behavior feeds bitterness and despair. A very common feeling in those who are overweight is the feeling of being insignificant and hopeless. In a world where young, hard bodies are paraded around for attention, it is easy to feel insignificant: "I really don't matter. I'm not *one of those.*" Hopelessness can come from struggling for the majority of your life to maintain a healthy weight. It sometimes seems as if the world revolves around thin people. For those with less-than-perfect bodies, this realization feeds a deep sense of isolation, which in turn feeds addiction: "Food is my comfort. It will not fail me." To have emotional health and a sense of well-being, we need to feel our lives hold value for something beyond our body images.

I have heard of women who use weight gain as a barrier to avoid relationships with men because they have been hurt, rejected, or abused in some form, and don't want to be put in that position again. They use weight to avoid dealing with something that has brought them pain in the past. This is another way of running, of filling a hole and controlling your surroundings. The first step to overcoming this problem is to surround yourself with a team of people who will support and encourage you to replace the negative beliefs you have toward yourself with positive ones. Formulating this team is, perhaps, the most critical part of the process. You will need to have contact with these people on a weekly basis, and sometimes this process can take years before change is seen. Changing an ingrained negative belief you have held about yourself throughout your life is extremely difficult. Here's a helpful formula that I've always believed in:

$$\text{change/recovery} = \text{consistency} + \text{time} + \text{grace}$$

Consistency throughout time is absolutely necessary, and grace is perhaps the most powerful force in the universe. Grace is what allows us to receive love even when we don't deserve it. It's the key component of the process that is essential for any form of recovery. Surround yourself with a team of supporters, and stay in touch with them regularly. Allow them to speak new and positive truths into your life.

You can't do it alone, in your own power. You must have God and the people He will use to work recovery in your life. These supporters will become God in the flesh to you during the recovery process. For most of my life, I've harbored negative beliefs and held a very low opinion of myself. It took years (it's still an ongoing process) for me to believe I'm a worthy person with good qualities, after having such a horrendous view of myself. And what I have experienced with others in recovery is that our addictions reinforce to us how wicked we are, how unworthy we are. At the core, addictive behaviors are a form of self-loathing. But the greatest impact on my transformation has come from the people in my close circle, those that God put around me. Consistently, over time, their positive influence began to override the negative tapes that had been playing over and over in my head for years. I felt *powerless* to believe positive things about myself, but my team taught me that God designed me to be who I am. God used them to help me believe what I couldn't believe about myself. In isolation, I don't see how I would have ever grown or changed. My opinion of myself would probably have sunk even lower.

Many of us have grown up with negative self-images. Maybe people around us have reinforced these negative self-images, fracturing our souls. For so many of us, this belief, this lie about ourselves, is so ingrained that it seems impossible to change. We're bombarded with these perfect-body images from the media, and we think, *That's what I'm going to do. That's what I'll control. My world will be controlled by this perfect body; then people will accept and admire me.* But that will never work. Ever. We must first believe in our inner beauty as God's children. We must see His faithfulness and love in our lives.

Compassion toward oneself is one of the most critical ingredients to the road to recovery. We're all going to make mistakes; that's inevitable. If we don't have compassion for ourselves, we'll be critical of others. Regardless of body type—obese, normal, too thin—we all tend to be extremely critical of others when we remain critical of ourselves. And we are all being influenced by this view of ourselves.

When I was addicted to maintaining my appearance as a control mechanism, I was working out three to four hours each day. Now that I'm free from this addiction, I don't have to worry about my appearance so much. There's nothing bad about feeling good about the way you look; if you work out to feel better and be healthier and you enjoy it, that's great! To enjoy what exercise does for your body is wonderful. But your body should not be the only reason for exercise. Exercise can provide physical, spiritual, and mental improvement. One way to involve the soul is to pray during your workout. You can experiment with ways to bring your spirit, mind, and body together.

Changing your body image ultimately comes down to the first beatitude, which is where the first of the twelve steps comes from: "Blessed are the poor in spirit." We need God's grace in order to change who we are, and to believe His truth about us: that we are beautiful creatures whom He loves. He wants us to believe this. After all, He is our creator; if we hold negative views of ourselves, we insult His creative design for each of us. When we see ourselves as unique created beings, our view of our physical selves changes.

We must come to believe this truth—that we are God's beloved children. Altering our self image is a process. There will be days of doubt—we've spent the majority of our lives doubting our acceptance in this world, and that's a hard habit to break. The process takes time. But day-by-day, situation by situation, your life can be changed.

REFLECTION QUESTIONS

What are some of the lies you believe about yourself?

Where do you think those lies are coming from?

If you were more accepting of yourself, how would it show? How would you act differently?

Write a positive affirmation about yourself.

Write a positive affirmation about yourself, as if it were coming from God. What would you want Him to say about you?

Name one person who you believe would support these affirmations about you.

REFLECTIONS

REFLECTIONS

REFLECTIONS

CHAPTER THREE

THE AFFIRMATION ADDICTION

A young woman, who had been battling bulimia for eight years as a teenager, came to Restore Ministries for help. Her problem began when a boy in her high school patted her belly and asked if she was pregnant. Never wanting to experience that kind of humiliation again, she began restricting her food intake and secretly purging. She once recounted a high school football game where she ate the ear off a Mickey Mouse ice cream bar, after having eaten nothing else all day, and then excused herself to go throw up in the stadium bathroom. She believed she needed to do this—that it was necessary to keep the body image she desired. She wanted to turn boys' heads and maintain their interest, but she was wasting away while seeking their approval.

Why do we need affirmation so much? The definition of *affirmation* is "maintain as true; assert positively; the assertion of the truth or existence of something; a positive statement."[1] When I receive affirmation, I believe it must mean something about me is positively true. When I am seeking affirmation, I want someone to tell me, "Scott, it's true. You have a quality that I admire. It's true that you're good; it's true that you're significant; it's true that you're attractive; it's true that I want to be near you." We're relying others to validate our significance. We think that if this recognition comes from someone else, perhaps it will make it true.

Is it possible to pursue affirmation in healthy ways? As long as we're seeking affirmation from others, and not from God, we are vulnerable. How can outward affirmation ever make us feel better inside if we can't control that affirmation? You can have a perfect body and still never get noticed. It's possible to look great and never hear, "Wow, you look terrific!" The harsh truth is that when we depend on others for our affirmation, sometimes it doesn't come. If we don't have positive internal beliefs about ourselves, we'll seek affirmation from others at all costs, even when the results are futile and destructive.

When we seek affirmation in dysfunctional ways, we feel insecure. A perfect example is the woman in the Bible who met Jesus at a well. She had been married multiple times, and yet the emptiness of her soul was apparent. Despite her attempts to find affirmation, she still felt unloved. In the same way, our desire for affirmation causes us to falsely believe that we must be attractive to be loved. When we look to the external and buy into the standard for beauty based on what the media has created, then we'll never be satisfied with our body images. Why? Because it's nearly impossible to match this standard. And this intense dissatisfaction with one's body can easily result in eating disorders.

This incessant need to find affirmation from others can become an addictive response. When I *need* something, it has a power over me that I cannot control. When I need you to affirm me—when my self-acceptance and self-love come from outside myself—then I am no longer in control. Once I believe I need someone else to tell me who I am, I begin to look for ways to get that affirmation. I begin to believe that I need to look a certain way, and if I look that way, then my deepest need—to be told that I'm loved as a human being—will be met.

I read an article in *More* magazine recently about a photographer who, in her quest to help women find contentment and joy in their bodies, is planning on doing a series of tasteful nude photographs. In many cases, the models are the photographer's own friends. There were some amazing quotes from these normal, average women on their longtime struggles to accept their bodies. One woman, named Gail, said:

> This vessel that I live in is basically healthy and strong. It's taken many years, but now when I look in the mirror, I feel gratitude and love. When I was in my teens, I was a constant dieter. I hated the size and shape of my breasts. I was frustrated by my hairy legs. I thought my nose was too long. The list of criticisms seemed endless. Now I have the same body, only it's older, saggier, and weighs about five pounds more, and I feel none of that self-loathing. Instead, I feel tenderness and gratitude for what this body can do and has done for me. I even think, "Pretty good for a 48-year-old."

Another woman, Stephanie, sees herself in a different light after finding a surprising new hobby:

> Every day, my body looks more like my mother's. Does everyone say that? Regular workouts don't seem to budge the steady coating of fat. I'd like to lose a lot of weight and gain a lot of muscle. I do triathlons; I would like to look like a triathlete. If you'd asked me ten years ago—when I was at least fifty pounds lighter—what I liked about my body, I would have said absolutely nothing. When people complimented me, I wondered what their motives were: They could not possibly believe what they were saying. Also, ten years ago, I would have never competed in a triathlon because I would not have been seen dead in the outfit you have to wear. Now I couldn't care less what I look like when I am competing.[2]

The only tragedy here is that all these women were in their forties before they began to accept their bodies. The enemy wants you to be disconnected from yourself. What I mean is that you can't love part of yourself and not another; it's inner discord. So if the enemy can accomplish that by making you hate your body, his work is halfway done, his first lie accepted. But God wants you to know the truth. He is saying, "I made you—all of you. Everything about you. And I love you." The journey to loving everything about yourself—your flaws and your gifts—is foundational. In my own personal journey of recovery, I needed to believe the truth that God loves me with all the mistakes that I've made, with all of my flaws. My relationship with God is central in my life, because I know He loves me unconditionally. The standard that I judge myself by is no longer coming from the world, but from God who created me.

Tilly's Story

The need to be loved, the desire to be beautiful, fueled every aspect of my obsession with my body. I thought that if I could just look perfect, then I would be perfect. If I could have the perfect body, somebody would desire me. This desire for someone to care for and comfort me ran all the way down to the core. I felt that if someone would just accept me, then I could stop this destructive cycle that I was on.

During this time in my life, I began to pursue a career in music. I was gifted with a voice and a desire to sing. It was my passion and a way to escape from everything else that consumed me. But the music industry is a tough field to be in when you are not comfortable with yourself in the first place. Everything is governed by appearance. Your look is what sells your music.

At the age of fifteen, I put out an independent jazz record. My parents sat me down and said they were worried about me. "You aren't . . . fat," my dad told me, "but you know those people who are sort of in-between? You're kind of like that." They were trying to protect me from the music industry—an industry that fed off of appearance. They were telling me what I was already telling myself: that half of a music career was appearance, and I should keep that in mind. Maybe even lose a little weight.

I'm sure that the next few years would have looked the same with or without that talk, but it still confirmed my worst fears about the way others saw me and, more important, the way that I saw myself. I drowned myself in my addiction for affirmation from others and specifically from boys. I finished school when I was fifteen, and at sixteen decided to go to college in town when they offered me a scholarship. I lost a little weight in my excitement about my upcoming life and the excitement of living away from home.

In college, I was overjoyed to be free. I was ready to begin again, with a fresh persona. I was an extremely friendly freshman. I learned to talk to boys. I was flirted with, and I flirted back. I was told that I was pretty. I fell in love for the first time—at least, as close to love as a seventeen-year-old could experience. I lived and breathed by what others thought about me. It meant absolutely everything to me.

Affirmation really does play a key role in the dysfunction of poor body image and issues with food. Most of us are addicted to seeking affirmation from others. We want to be respected and admired by those of the same gender, and we also seek a different kind of admiration from those of the opposite gender.

It's perfectly normal to want to be desired by the opposite sex, is it not? It always feels good to be told you're beautiful or handsome or desired. If a woman flirts with me, it sends a signal of affirmation: "Something about you is desirable." When we receive signals that we are desired, it feels good, doesn't it? But this affirmation needs to be put in the proper perspective. It's like a nice stroke on the back. But when we become dependant on it for our sense of well-being and self-worth, we're in trouble.

As human beings, we were created with a need for a certain kind of affirmation. It has been shown again and again that people cannot survive without love from other people. In orphanages during WWII, the babies were all fed regularly, but not all of them were held and cuddled. Most of those who were held were able to survive and even thrive despite wartime conditions. But those that were fed sufficiently but not held every day died.[3] We are literally born with a need to be loved.

Most of the affirmation we get from others is conditional. Very often, people admire us if we look a certain way or perform a certain way. It's conditional. But the affirmation that comes from God's love is unconditional. It's not based on how we look, or what we achieve. It's based on who we are in Him, and nothing can ever take His love away. If I never achieve anything in my life, if I never look the way I'd like, God's love will still be there. Affirmation from other sources will always be conditional—that's why the need for this kind of affirmation feeds into eating disorders and obesity.

We crave this conditional, worldly affirmation because, deep down, we are self-absorbed. After all, this type of affirmation is all about us—it's dependent on our own achievements. But God's love has nothing to do with how beautiful or charming or admirable we are. It's all about Him. He gives despite our flaws; He fills in for our weakness.

When a woman dresses provocatively, and has a "sexy" body, she's certain to receive certain affirmations from the world. But these have absolutely no depth. She will always need more.

Marilyn Monroe has long been considered one of the loveliest among women. You could say she died of a broken heart—famous and empty. Anna Nicole Smith tried to control her world through the way she looked—but it ultimately failed her. People were fascinated with her and talked about her, but she was very alone. Both of these women died tragically, drowning in private misery. According to the world's message, they—beautiful and famous—should have been among the happiest of people. Why do we seek this kind of affirmation so aggressively? Because we know we need *something*.

There are certain symptoms that usually come with an addiction to affirmation, and one of the most prominent is isolation. With the inherent desire for affirmation comes an inherent fear of rejection, which leads to isolation. We feed our loneliness with food, anger, or self-loathing, and we do this in emotional solitude. We do need affirmation from others. If our parents don't tell us they love us, that they're proud of us, then we will likely feel that sting for years, if not the rest of our lives. Verbal neglect is a common experience of many of the people who come to Restore Ministries.

Another symptom of addiction to affirmation is body perfectionism. Our society has created the illusion that a perfect body equals love and happiness. Does losing weight affect the life of a morbidly obese person? Certainly. It has the potential to make that person healthier and happier and it can enable him to live more fully. Your body is part of who you are, so your physical health is important. But your body is not your whole self, and there's a difference between health and cosmetics.

But if you're seeking body perfection, you will always encounter dissatisfaction, which can lead to other issues—despair, despondence, binging, or starving. We must learn to accept and love our bodies for what they are—a gift. The human body is an amazing creation or wonder. It's the vessel that we are privileged to live in for our brief time here on earth, and it carries us around to experience what God has for us in this life. The body is not the means to the end that so many of us make it out to be. It is not a way to earn love, but rather a tool to accomplish what God has set before us. And, yes, we need to take care of it. One way we do that is to like it.

Yet another symptom of affirmation addiction is susceptibility to emotional affairs. Left unchecked, those emotional affairs can grow into full-blown physical affairs. An emotional affair can occur when we seek affirmation from the opposite sex. These affairs of the heart are driven by a need to have someone tell us that we are valued, attractive, and desired. Once we are addicted to the feeling this affirmation gives us, we want more and more. Affirmation can become like a drug, and even married people are not immune to its powers.

THE IMPORTANCE OF SUPPORT

Please don't misinterpret this chapter. I am not saying that we don't need other people to affirm us and tell us we are loved. As a wife, you're not addicted to affirmation if you want your husband to tell you that he loves you. As a husband, it's natural to want your wife to let you know that she thinks you're strong and capable. We do need affirmation—but the right kind and from the right sources.

In my own journey, I tended to enter relationships with females from a place of my own insecurity. What did I bring to the table? Appearance. That's it. And once the high of receiving a woman's affirmation wore off, I sought it elsewhere. That destructive pattern ruled my life for a long time. I see that same pattern again and again in men and women who come to Restore Ministries.

The people in my support group were the key to my recovery. They were able to speak truth into my life when I could not believe it for myself. There was no other place where I consistently received positive affirmation about who I was. Elsewhere, I was receiving destructive input about my flaws and weaknesses. It almost destroyed me with depression.

What are the differences between this addictive affirmation from random people and the positive affirmation from a circle of supporters? Besides providing a positive voice, a support group provides a safe environment where we can all be honest, real, and transparent. Outside a group, we might be tempted to live a false life, disguising our flaws. Within the group, we are affirmed—flaws and all—so there's no need to pretend. A good support group will exhibit the grace and mercy that comes from God. Choosing this group is one of the most significant steps in your recovery process. Be sure that each person in the group has these four critical qualities: they must be safe, they must be supportive and visionary, they must be encouraging, and they must be willing to keep you accountable.

These visionaries are absolutely essential to your recovery. They will help you to see the positive and to believe it. Without a vision, it's easy to accept less. There's a saying in sports that you will only play up to the level of your opponent. It's easier for a bad team to pull a good team down to its level than it is for the good team to pull a bad team up to theirs. But when you see two excellent teams play each other, they play at an unbelievable level.

When I spend time with people who are encouraging, they pull me up to their level. The type of people we surround ourselves with will often define who we are. But surrounding yourself with encouraging people with strong personal values might make you uncomfortable at first. I don't mean that you'll face judgment—remember, they must be safe to qualify for your support group—but the sensation will be new if you're used to surrounding yourself with mediocre people.

It's human nature to gravitate toward people we have common ground with. If we surround ourselves with people who are supportive, or at least tolerant, of our addictions, we'll remain at their level. But when we surround ourselves with positive people who will push us to greater things, we'll be pulled up, out of the mire of addiction. The people we surround ourselves with play a huge role in recovery. Choose your friends and support group wisely.

We all desire to be affirmed, because ultimately affirmation is expressing that we are loved. That's at the heart of human desire. But as long as we seek that affirmation outside of our relationship with God, it will never fill us. Just like the old song says, we're "looking for love in all the wrong places." Jesus said it to the woman at the well, but He could have been talking to us in the twenty-first century: *What you're seeking is not in those places. You will only find it with Me.*

REFLECTION QUESTIONS

What is your real motivation for working out?

What kind of people are you spending your time with? Are they able to love you with the love of Christ?

What adjectives do you think God would use to describe you?

What positive comments or compliments from others have you disregarded in the past week? Why do you think you dismissed those comments?

What masks do you wear to conceal your true self?

Where do you go, and to whom do you go to, for love and affirmation?

REFLECTIONS

REFLECTIONS

REFLECTIONS

CHAPTER FOUR

LIFE AS A FOOD ADDICT

A 2003 article in *Guideposts* tells the story of Jan Bono, a woman with a severe food addiction who struggled for years with obesity. In her story, Jan gives a heartfelt testimony about her experience. Jan's eating was out of control, but she didn't know how to change it. She was stuck in the vortex of her addiction, feeling isolated. This is how she described herself:

"I was 45 years old, five foot six and weighed 396 pounds. The only clothes that fit me were size 60 blouses and voluminous elastic-waist paints. My shoes all had Velcro straps; I couldn't reach my feet to tie laces. I had recently bought a new full size car because it was the only one whose steering wheel I could fit behind. I was miserable. Yet I couldn't admit it to anyone. I couldn't even talk about it."

Her problems, she says, started in early childhood. "As far back as I can remember I loved to sneak. Mom made big batches of chocolate chip cookies for our family of six and stored them in bags in the freezer. I'd take a bunch and hide them in my room. Whatever was bothering me, however happy or sad or bored I felt, gorging myself always helped, as if I could fill up a sense of emptiness inside. Even when I was a child, my eating was dishonest." In college, Jan devoured cookie dough or bags of cookies when her roommate wasn't around. "I hid food like an alcoholic hides booze." She often made stops at several different restaurants around town so that no one would know how much she was consuming.[1]

The patterns are the same as with other addictions that we address at Restore Ministries—hiding, secrecy, isolation. Mike O'Neil, author of *Power to Choose*, says it this way: "We're only as sick as our secrets."

Marriage couldn't fix the problem Jan had with food. She went through a painful divorce and slipped into depression. She was trapped in a cycle of failed diets and emotional eating. As a middle school teacher, she dealt with the terrible antics of her students. She was frequently called "fatso" and "whale" behind her back. Sinking in depression, having failed miserably at every diet she undertook, Jan sought the help of a therapist.

The counselor recommended that she find a support group for people who struggled with overeating. In fact, the therapist was so adamant that she refused to work with Jan until she went to a support group for twelve meetings. Jan reluctantly found and joined a group. On the first day, she told them her name was Sylvia and even lied about her age. She didn't speak or participate in the group. She couldn't be her true self, even in a support group full of overeaters.

Then she heard someone talk about receiving "God's help" for the addiction. She writes, "God's help . . . I was sure that God could not help me." Hearing others talk about the support of loved ones and God was beyond her comprehension, since food was her only friend. Instead of support, she only knew isolation, shame, rejection, and lies.

Near the end of the twelve weeks, some kids shouted "moooo" behind her as she walked down a hallway. A thought of sharing this humiliation with her support group came to mind, but she rejected the thought. Instead, she thought about the sandwich in her purse and how she would eat the pain away. She felt hopeless and believed that nothing in her life would ever change, that there was no hope for her in this addiction.

After her second last meeting with the support group, she got in her car and cried out accusingly to God that He could never help her and never would. It was the deepest moment of isolation and loneliness she'd ever experienced. When she arrived at home there was a package for her. Inside was a flat polished rock with a single word engraved on it: *Hope*. She placed that rock in the center of her table and she didn't want to eat. That rock stood between her and her addiction to food. This was the beginning of her recovery.

At her last group meeting, she wasn't ashamed to speak. With encouragement from her peers and God's encouragement, she realized that she was not alone. She confessed that her name was not Sylvia, that it was Jan, and said, "I am really glad to be here."

She stepped into the community of supportive people and a loving God, and her healing began. She lost 231 pounds.[2]

Food has always been a socially accepted drug. If you're an alcoholic or drug addict, there's a good chance you'll eventually suffer some severe consequences. You might lose your job or possibly face legal troubles. If you drive a car irresponsibly, you'll get arrested and maybe lose your license or go to jail. Society doesn't condone this sort of behavior. But if you eat until you're stuffed, over and over again, the consequences are subtler. You'll keep your job and your driver's license. Nobody will come take your children away. In fact, you'll find that society often supports your habit. There are no commercials or ads that I'm aware of that try to lure you into taking drugs. But there are countless tantalizing ads on TV and in magazines that entice us to eat.

Our culture fosters addictive responses to food. It is no wonder that so many of us are obese. Think about this: an addict uses drugs to fill loneliness, emptiness, pain, and anxiety—and food is the easiest drug to obtain. We're reminded of food at every turn—vending machines, fast-food restaurants, advertisements, grocery stores, movie theaters. Food is everywhere! Our society encourages addictions to food, and yet it doesn't condone obesity. Anorexia and bulimia are real issues that shouldn't be accepted in our society either—but someone who is too thin is not ostracized the same way an obese person often is.

One thing we know about addiction is that there is a parental link. Some believe addiction is in our genes, but many obese parents pass it

on to their children by modeling it. Obesity is a multi-generational epi-
demic, and we live in a society full of food addicts. The very idea of
addiction means that we can't stop doing something, even when it's
unhealthy. Alcoholics can't stop at one or two drinks. They need more
and more, and their tolerance keeps growing. Likewise, the food addict
keeps eating and eating, but stays hungry. I'm not referring to the phys-
iological aspect of the stomach stretching. Emotionally, the appetite
grows. The food addict needs more and more to satisfy the hunger.
Eventually—just like the alcoholic who must drink all the time—the
food addict either eats or wants to eat constantly.

Tilly's Story

Somewhere in the midst of all this commotion in my new college
life, I began to abandon my restrictive diet and to eat compulsively
as a way to cover up my emotions and hide my pain. My parents' marriage had been on the rocks for a while, and I made feeble attempts
to try and shelter my five siblings from the insanity that was wreck-
ing havoc on our home. So I hid myself in food. The summer after my
freshman year in college was filled with lots of eating and depression.
I gained more than I would have liked over that summer.

As I went into sophomore year, I was overwhelmed with depression
and friend and boyfriend complications. Eventually, every night was a
food fest. Sometimes it was with friends, but a lot of the time, I was
alone. I had rituals for eating, like any food addict. I would take little
things from roommates who had offered their food in the past, and then
I would visit any free-food events on campus that didn't require too
much time in public. I would make multiple visits to the snack
machines in the dorm, or one visit to the cafeteria, sometimes using up
two meals under the pretension that I was getting food for someone
else. I should have, by all accounts, been morbidly obese at that time.

But because of my compulsive eating, I also had enormous amounts of guilt. So I would work out rigidly enough that my weight gain was slow. But I could see it on myself. I was so disgusted once again with myself that the pain only grew. Mirrors, shopping, or anything that would remind me of food, would not only make me hate myself but would make me desire the food more. I was so embarrassed, and it seemed there was nothing that I could do. I was in way over my head.

In the middle of my sophomore year, I read a few books and articles on eating disorders, and, finally accepting the fact that I would never find the willpower to be anorexic, I wondered about bulimia. No part of me wanted to really become bulimic, but I was curious. One day, after a particularly sickening bout of eating, as I sat and groaned to myself, hating the way I felt at the moment and hating who I was, I decided to see if I could throw up. I hadn't thrown up, even with the flu, since the age of maybe ten or eleven. But I did that day. And the next week. It never really gave the sense of having "made it better," of having atoned for my overeating, as I hoped for, but it took away the edge. In moments of feeling ill from my overeating, I purged several times. I was miserable and completely consumed. Food was controlling my life.

We all know that food is a powerful and pleasurable experience. It can even create a mood-altering affect. Some of us have deep-rooted emotional attachments to high sugar and fat foods—foods we call the "C" foods—cookies, candy, cake, chips.

In an early part of Jan's story she said, "But food does change things for me. It is my friend."[3] This is an authentic perspective for the relationship—so many of us have with food. It fills us with a sense of pleasure when we are sad. It offers a sense of comfort when we're empty. We have memories of favorite foods and the pleasure they have given us. These emotional associations with food make it easy to fall into an addictive response. Food is the most socially addictive drug, and it's also socially acceptable.

Sex addictions and food addictions are rooted in the pleasure center of the brain. These are probably the two most pleasurable experiences God gave us. We were created to enjoy food as well as sex. But our relationship with food or sex becomes toxic when it crosses the line beyond being something we enjoy, to being something we need, something that shields us from being lonely, tired, or sad. We have to eat to live, but we shouldn't live to eat. The key to recovery is becoming free from the obsession with food, from craving food when our bodies are not hungry. We need to understand the difference between physical hunger and emotional or spiritual hunger.

Jan believes her binges with food were an attempt to fill emptiness.[4] This is common for almost every addiction—we believe that the addiction can fill up our emptiness. One man in Jan's support group said, "I realized that overeating wouldn't really change anything."[5]

If we seek out our drug of choice when we're feeling down and lonely, it may give us a temporary feeling of comfort. But inevitably feelings of self-contempt follow, because we have once again caved in and "used," as we say in recovery. Only then do we realize that our addictions don't change the emptiness. They might create a mood-altering feeling, but it is always followed by a deep swing toward despair: *I've fed this addiction. I've failed again.* Recognizing the cycle of addiction is one of the steps in defeating it. Every addiction begins with the obsession with our drug of choice. Often, the obsession is triggered by a sequence of events that leads to denial. In one of our Restore Ministries groups, I asked, "What is denial?" The first person who responded said, "It means you're unable to see the truth." A second participant gave a more accurate definition: "It's a *refusal* to see the truth." Denial is a mental block, a way of protecting ourselves from a painful reality we don't want to embrace. Instead, we refuse to see it.

I've worked with alcoholics who have been arrested for multiple DUIs and been to jail. Yet at the time, these men and women didn't believe they had a problem with alcohol. As I went to pick them up from jail or visit them behind bars, they would still insist that it was just bad luck that they were caught. Addicts believe they are in control of their addictions. Denial allows us to shift blame to someone else or a set of circumstances. It gives us permission to do what we really want to do. As long as you're in denial, *nothing's going to change.* Jan was a great example: she was willing to go to counseling but was unwilling to take steps beyond that, denying that she needed help.

It's nearly impossible to emerge from denial on our own. We need help from two sources. First and foremost, we need God. "Nothing in all the world can be hidden from God. Everything is clear and lies open before him, and to him we must explain the way we have lived" (Heb. 4:13 NCV). We can never hide in denial before God. He sees. We might refuse to look at our food addictions, but God's Spirit will expose the truth to us if we allow Him. He'll never pressure us, but when we turn to Him, He will give us the strength to overcome any addiction. "You gave me strength in battle" (Ps. 18:39 NCV). So ask God for help.

It wasn't until I got into a Christ-centered addiction program that God revealed the truth to me. It was the beginning of my liberation. As we say in group, "Discovery leads to recovery." God brings what is hidden to light, so that He can fix it. "He will bring to light things that are now hidden in darkness, and will make known the secret purposes of people's hearts" (1 Cor. 4:5 NCV).

We also need other people to help us out of denial. God uses His people to lovingly speak truth into our lives. It's easy to get defensive with a spouse or friend who is criticizing our flaws. We all have a desire to please, and knowing we have failed is hard to accept. But in the safe environment of a recovery group, the goal is to face the truth of your behavior. I get calls regularly from people who will not listen to their families about their addiction, but they want to hear correction from me. In recovery groups you'll hear from people who share your same struggles and who have no ulterior motives. God can sometimes use these people more effectively than those who are closest to us.

As I've mentioned before, denial and isolation are intertwined. Through denial, we stay isolated in a defensive hiding place. Take Jan, for example.

As long as she was in denial, she refused to acknowledge her truth, even to those in her group. Many of us, like Jan, know that if we stay in denial we can continue to medicate our pain with our addictions. But once we confront the truth and share it with others, we know we'll be encouraged to fight the addiction, to give up our drugs of choice.

Jan felt that food was her only friend, and this realization brought about a sense of hopelessness. The only antidote to hopelessness is hope. When we believe there is hope, we can stop denying the existence of our addictions. We can reach out for help because hope is the catalyst for perseverance and recovery. Romans 15:13 says, "I pray that the God who gives hope will fill you with much joy and peace while you trust in him. Then your hope will overflow by the power of the Holy Spirit" (NCV).

There's a scene in the movie *Parenthood* in which a wife is rejected by her husband. She goes into her closet and opens a box filled with junk food—Twinkies, cookies, etc.—and she starts wolfing it down. This is a great example of isolation and medication.

Isolation is a natural tendency for many of us. We've been doing it since Adam and Eve hid in the garden. "I heard you walking in the garden, and I was afraid because I was naked, so I hid" (Gen. 3:10 NCV). Shame drives us to isolate, to hide so that people don't know where we are. As my friend Dr. Chip Dodd says, when God called out to Adam He wasn't asking where Adam was physically. He was asking, "Where are you? In your heart, in your soul—where have you wandered off to? Why have you wandered away from me, and why are you hiding from me?"

There are so many reasons people hide—fear of rejection, shame, guilt, fear of retribution. Hiding is taking the easy path. But stepping into the light, into accountability and honesty—even stepping into hope— takes courage. It's hard to say, "I'm struggling. I'm alone. I'm afraid you'll reject me." But if we never come out of hiding, then we will never truly love or be loved.

It's hard to take a good, honest look at ourselves when we're in isolation. Isolation is a fertile soil for addictions to grow, and for the roots to get deeper and stronger. Coming out of isolation and living in the light and the presence of God, with His Spirit leading us into truth, enables us to achieve freedom from addiction.

BEGINNING THE PROCESS

Recovery from food addiction requires ending certain behaviors and initiating new ones. First, we must make peace with God, peace with ourselves, and peace with others. This is the heart of the twelve-step process. When we're at peace, we can grow into new creatures with new approaches to living. God transforms us from the inside out, producing new relationships with food and our bodies. Old, destructive patterns change, and we become different; we have different friends, different lifestyles, different goals. We no longer crave affirmation to feel good about our bodies.

Recovery should involve many new things—new friends, new environments, and new food choices. This won't happen overnight; it's a process that will take time. Remember the formula: recovery = consistency + time + grace. Be compassionate and gracious toward yourself. You're not striving for perfection—you want progress. You might take two steps forward, and then one step back. You will have setbacks and slips, times when you fall back into a previous pattern. There's a difference between a brief slip and a major, full-blown relapse. In a full-blown relapse, an addict returns to his previous lifestyle with no intentions to rebound.

Build your program for change around God and the people supporting you. Know that you can change with God's help and the help of others. Say good-bye to old habits and replace them with new, healthier habits.

THE BOTTOM LINE

As a food addict, you won't instantly get to a place where you say, "No thanks. I'm not hungry. I'll eat only when I'm hungry and stop immediately when I'm full." The plan for recovery is the same as it is for an alcoholic, drug addict, sex addict, or any other addict. The first step is to come out of isolation and find a community. Come out of hiding and begin to build awareness of your issues. Invite God into the inner recesses of your heart and ask, "What void am I trying to fill with food? What am I trying to obtain through my obsession with food and my body? What am I trying to control?"

Get into a twelve-step program and apply it to your issue. Keep things in the light, stay connected to people, and develop new habits with food. When you come out of denial you'll discover that food has been your god, your comforter, your obsession. Don't wallow in the shame of failure, and forgive yourself for momentary slips or setbacks. When you do relapse, go to your accountability person or group. Identify what caused the setback (stress, fear, loneliness, rebellion), and formulate a plan to handle the situation if it comes up again.

Christ has the ability to change us, to transform us, so that our relationships with food will change. Our relationships with our body will change, too, if we stay on course. Use relapses for good, and know that it does get easier, that cravings and binges do dissipate over time. Ultimately, when you're fully encapsulated in your new life, you can look back and say, "Wow, how did I get that way?"

Be encouraged that God will do for you what you cannot do for yourself. He will use this journey to transform your entire life. Let this hope give you an intrinsic motivation to pursue your new life. You are in the process of working with God to make a new self, and this new self will have a new and different relationship with food and its body. As time goes by, the urgings and cravings will diminish. Be encouraged by this! If you work through your recovery process, it will work for you. You *will* find freedom.

REFLECTION QUESTIONS

What impact has your relationship with food had on your life?

If a "truth mirror" were held in front of you, would you be able to look? What do you think you would see?

How many signs or messages of encouragement has God sent you this week? What form did they take? Were you receptive to them?

What setbacks or barriers do you expect to encounter when you begin making changes? Rather than giving in or giving up, what adjustments can you make to stay on track?

Jesus said He came that we might have life abundantly. If you allowed Him to have all of your heart and life, what would your "abundant life" be like?

REFLECTIONS

Why do I want to change.
A good reflection for me is to
encorporate exercise in my
daily plan. I believe this will
help me to lose the excess weight
I am trying to lose. Also, watch
my portion in eating my food
and count calories for a
better outcome.

REFLECTIONS

CHAPTER FIVE

CREATING A NEW LIFESTYLE

Bookstores have shelves lined with books about diet and exercise, each promising that if we follow their plans—only eat raw foods, shun carbohydrates, eliminate white flour, or whatever the latest trend is—we'll be healthy and content. But we can't change ourselves from the inside out by diet and exercise alone. Sure, the people on the book covers or in the ads are fit and perfect—that's good advertising. But in reality, most of us will never look like perfect cover models. We need to come to grips with this reality as we journey toward a healthy body image.

A healthy body image begins with a new lifestyle. It starts inside first, and then works its way to the outward appearance. Once we begin to receive our affirmation from God, as we learned in an earlier chapter, it changes us on the inside. If we develop a healthy relationship with food, it creates enthusiasm as we see our body image change. Affirmation fuels our new lifestyle, giving us a new sense of well-being. If we can maintain our enthusiasm and motivation as we pursue inward transformation, we'll begin to see changes in our physical and emotional health.

In her book, *The Artist's Way*, Julia Cameron discusses creativity, a close relative to enthusiasm. "Creativity" encompasses passion, fun, joy, and, ultimately, enthusiasm. Cameron writes, "Over an extended period of time, being an artist requires enthusiasm more than discipline. Enthusiasm is not an emotional state. It is a spiritual commitment, a loving surrender to our creative process, a loving recognition of all the creativity around us."[1]

Our new lifestyle creates enthusiasm, which is different from maintaining discipline. Discipline says, "I have to do this." So you dig your heels in and just do it. Enthusiasm, on the other hand, says, "I want to do this." Our motivation flows and prompts us to do it. This paradigm shift from discipline to enthusiasm is the new lifestyle we must embrace—an active lifestyle with a healthy relationship with food.

Tilly's Story

My sister's wedding was actually the beginning of my recovery. I was still broken, still wondering how I could feel the way I felt about life. I was still essentially a wreck. But her wedding truly pushed me over the edge. Two weeks before the wedding, my best guy friend professed his undying love for me, and I, unable to return the sentiment, felt terrible. The only way that I knew how to deal with that pain was to restrict and to purge, telling myself it was because I was trying to look perfect for my sister's wedding. I threw up almost every day for a few weeks, trying desperately to make myself feel better. Finally I dragged myself into my parents' bedroom and told them about this thing, this addiction that I had been hiding for years.

They had never had any personal experience with eating disorders, but they desperately wanted to help me and be there for me. They comforted, supported, and encouraged me the best way they knew how. But just the fact that someone else knew, that I had finally shared this pain with someone, made it bearable for a time. I did not magically in that moment become healed, nor did I walk away from that conversation feeling as though my parents truly thought that "I was beautiful," but I walked away knowing that I made the first step. I had finally reached out and was not rejected, but embraced.

LET'S DO SOME CARDIO!

If I were to design a fitness plan for you, it would consist of three parts: cardiovascular fitness, strength training, and nutrition. (Most people focus on the nutritional aspect of things, but I believe the other two are at least as—if not more—important. We'll discuss nutrition in the next chapter.) When you become active, it strengthens your cardiovascular system and causes the body to release endorphins. This workout provides a natural form of relaxation for your body. You sleep better and think better. You are calmer. Endorphins slow down the speed of your body's aging processes and keep your joints and muscles working and strong. God created humans to be active, to be mobile, and to have physical exertion. Personally, I love the feeling of going for a good, brisk walk. Then, after a hot shower that relaxes me, my brain calms down and I'm more able to focus. I have a sense of well-being, and this is when I do my best writing, my best work, my best conversing, and my best communion with God. I believe increasing activity is the most important aspect of a fitness plan.

Fitness guru Jack LaLanne once said, "Exercise is King. Nutrition is Queen. Put them together and you've got a kingdom."[2] This is a great way to express the hierarchy of exercise above nutrition.

The cardiovascular element of my fitness plan includes aerobic activity such as walking, stationary biking, aerobics, water aerobics, dancing, and swimming. Aerobic means "with oxygen," so any activity that causes you to move and exert continuous energy, increasing the body's need for oxygen, is considered aerobic. Our bodies were meant to move, so choose an activity you enjoy—one that will make it easier to stay enthused about and stick with it. I'm personally an advocate of walking, since almost everybody enjoys it and you can control the intensity by altering your pace. Walking is safe for just about everyone, you can socialize with friends while you walk, and you can do it almost anywhere. It's stimulating and provides a great opportunity for deep thought, meditation, or prayer.

It's essential that you choose an aerobic activity you enjoy and will look forward to doing. Walking creates enthusiasm for me. I enjoy being outside. I love seeing the trees, the lake, the sun, the birds, all of nature. I can walk in cold weather or warm weather, and I enjoy the changing seasons. I also use my walking time to pray or talk to loved ones. If you don't enjoy being outdoors, most YMCAs or other health facilities have indoor tracks or treadmills, and your local mall is a great place to walk as well—just don't let window-shopping distract you from your workout.

The length of your walk will depend on your level of fitness, but thirty minutes at a nice, brisk pace is usually adequate for most people. Get your heart rate up at some point along the walk. You can do this by altering your speed or the terrain (a hill, for example). For optimum health, try to walk or do some type of cardio workout every day.

When I am unable to take my daily walk, I truly miss it. I feel like a better person when I walk—mentally alert and more energetic. But if you enjoy more intensity, try running, swimming, or aerobics. Just remember to you enjoy whatever you're doing. You can never underestimate enthusiasm.

You can incorporate spiritual exercise into your cardio time as well. I take a quote or a Bible verse on an index card to meditate on as I walk. I call these my "power" walks because God strengthens me physically through my exercise and spiritually through His Word. When you think on nothing but a particular Scripture passage for thirty to sixty minutes, you're going to remember it. It will impact you! One of my favorites is, "I can do all things through Christ who strengthens me"

(Phil. 4:13 NKJV). I use this one when I'm struggling with self-confidence or temptation with my addictions.

A good walk is also helpful in fighting depression. Studies have shown that aerobic activity, three times a week, can have the same anti-depressant effects as a moderate dose of prescription anti-depressants.[3]

STRENGTH TRAINING

The second part of my fitness plan includes weight lifting. For years, when I was the senior wellness director at the Green Hills YMCA in Nashville, Tennessee, I was helping people develop their own fitness programs. I did seminars every late winter or early spring—the time when people start to think about bathing suit weather—for a wellness program called "Spring into Shape." The goal of the program was to help the members focus on ways to reduce body fat. In doing research for my presentation, I found numerous resources supporting the immense benefits of strength training. Whether you're eighteen or eighty, you need some form of strength training.

Strength training vastly improves your metabolism, which is the rate at which you burn calories while at rest. The higher the resting metabolic rate, the more calories we burn when we're at rest. Since most of us don't exercise all day every day (in fact, the majority of us are sedentary—including sleeping time—for at least twenty hours a day), resting metabolism is an important element in weight loss. Some sources say that muscle burns twice as many calories at rest as fat does. Others say that one pound of fat burns two calories per day, while one pound of muscle burns fourty to sixty calories per day.[4] In either case, it is clear that strength training increases your resting metabolism, allowing you to burn more calories at rest.

Strength training also strengthens your joints, helps maintain bone density (which helps prevent osteoporosis), and helps regulate blood sugar. As we get older, sugary meals are especially hard on the body because the sugar converts to fat. Think of your body as a car. A big engine needs more fuel than a small one. Muscles are what move our bodies and require fuel. If we're sedentary, then our muscle mass deteriorates, causing our "vehicle" to slow its burn rate significantly. A body with little muscle mass can go all day with very little fuel. But when we feed this small engine as if it were a big, muscular one, the extra energy gets converted to fat.

When people live interactive lifestyles, they lose muscle mass, their metabolisms slow, and they gain weight. Here in America, we usually diet first to fix the problem. But once you slow caloric intake, metabolism also slows, exacerbating the problem. When a person diets, most of the weight loss is muscle and water. When they return to their normal eating patterns, they often gain back the same weight and often more. Ninety-five percent of dieters regain all the weight they've lost.[5]

No matter your age, you can benefit greatly from strength training. We know from numerous researchers that you can build muscle at any age. By continuing to build muscle, your body will have a higher resting metabolic rate, so you will burn more calories at rest and become healthier and more lean. I believe that strength training is vital to your overall well-being, and it also has a great impact on you losing weight or maintaining your weight. Muscle burns almost twice as many calories at rest than fat does. So, as we get older and if we are inactive, our metabolism will slow down and we will gain weight. Even if your eating less will not help you lose weight.

For women, who naturally have less muscle, strength training is even more important than for men. It doesn't matter how old you are—you will benefit from becoming active and from strength training. I'm fifty-two, and lifelong strength training has preserved me.

REFLECTION QUESTIONS

This chapter offered several health tips. Which can you start putting into practice today?

What does becoming more spiritually active mean to you? What would you have to do to become closer to God?

What in your life are you enthusiastic about? Explain.

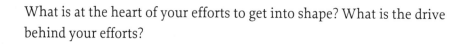

What is at the heart of your efforts to get into shape? What is the drive behind your efforts?

Describe your eating habits. (How many times a day do you eat? What are you eating? How much are you eating?)

Do you feel you need to change your eating habits? What, specifically, do you think needs to change?

Do you harbor any secret eating patterns that you don't want anyone to know about? If so, would you be willing to admit them now and write about them below?

REFLECTIONS

REFLECTIONS

REFLECTIONS

CHAPTER SIX

THE PURSUIT OF FREEDOM

Unhealthy relationships with our bodies and with food are crippling lives across the country. Many of us are so obsessed with how we look that we live in a constant state of dissatisfaction. This dissatisfaction becomes a chronic companion that distracts us from living to the fullest.

We need a totally different approach to what the diet culture of America would have us do. Instead of focusing on body fat and trying to lose it in order to gain some control over our lives, we should focus on a lifestyle that gives us the energy to pursue purpose in life.

George Bernard Shaw wrote, "Youth is wasted on the young."[1] I do see Mr. Shaw's point, because it often takes years of experience to find our purpose or niche in this life. Oh, to have the energy of youth and the wisdom that comes with age! But I'm very passionate about inspiring people to take advantage of the later seasons in life—it's not too late to do something great! When I look at my life and my career over the years, I realize that I am just beginning to do what I was born to do. I have found my purpose in life, with God's help, and am embarking on new experiences every day. We need to take care of these earthly bodies God has given us so that we'll have the strength to take on new challenges, even in advanced age.

Tilly's Story

I have made great strides in conquering my eating disorder and dealing with my need for the perfect body. The purging was easy to give up, because I never really wanted to do that, but the obsessing, the hating my body, has been much harder to give up. I have to say that it is an everyday decision. I still work out, and I still watch what I eat. But I do it because I want to be healthy now, not because I am fighting for control. Sometimes I still obsess over my reflection in a mirror and sometimes I don't, but that is all a part of the process of my recovery. Every day I am learning and every day I am growing. I have learned that I will never be "perfect" but I can be "great."

I want to be the best that I can be and I am learning the boundaries that I need to keep me healthy and safe. The restrictive diets don't work. The obsessive over-exercising won't fix anything either. But I love walking and hiking and just being active. I am loving life now, and I don't need anybody to tell me that they approve what I look like. Even though I am a woman and I want a relationship with a man, I don't need it to feel loved. God has given me so much to be thankful for, and I just continue to feed on that. He has become my focus and my energy for life. I am still singing and still continuing my journey. One day I hope to be completely free from my addiction to food and my body. As of today, I am one day closer.

GOOD NUTRITION

The third component of my health plan is nutrition. Because I'm sure there's nothing I can tell you that you haven't already heard, I am going to give you the most simple, honest approach to nutrition that you'll ever read. But I believe this simple approach will provide the basic foundations for enjoying a healthy relationship with food.

First, the bottom line is that you must make wise food choices. We all have foods that we love, we each have our own individual tastes, and so I don't like the idea of giving you a menu. I believe it's too restrictive for me to say, "These are the foods you must eat." However, I will say that when you choose, choose wisely. Below are some basic tips.

Choose whole grains over processed ones—pick foods made with whole-wheat flour instead of white, and choose brown rice instead of white rice. Look for the words "100 Percent Whole Grain" or something similar, as many products that are marketed as "wheat" are merely made from enriched, colored white flour. Whole grains have more nutritional value and are denser, which causes them to release energy more slowly, fill you up completely, and not mess around with your blood sugar levels.

Watch your intake of simple carbohydrates, such as white sugar and white flour. That includes almost anything that falls into the "junk food" category—candy, cookies, cake, and sugary soft drinks. These foods are very often the ones that food addicts crave, as they easily trigger the pleasure center of the brain. They're the foods most of us reach for when we're stressed or having a bad day. When you think of soothing a person with food, you would never say, "Hey, you've had a bad day. Sit down and let me get you some carrot and celery sticks. That'll make you feel better." No. Everyone knows what their own comfort foods are—and they're almost never healthy. When I'm feeling stressed and I want to medicate with food, I want a cheeseburger and fries, or a pepperoni pizza, or a big plate of hot cookies and milk. I might even pull into Krispy Kreme when the "hot" light is on.

For some, avoiding "comfort" foods altogether may be the best way to curb those cravings. Others might feel that allowing themselves small, infrequent portions of these foods keeps them from overindulging at another time. Whatever works for you is fine, but know that your food choices will affect the bottom line: your weight and your health.

For good nutrition, you also need to understand the difference between good fats and bad fats. We know that saturated fat—basically, animal fat—in large amounts is unhealthy. Saturated fat is found in meat, butter, and whole diary products. Does that mean we should go vegan? Not necessarily. Try reaching for leaner cuts of meat choices. There are plenty of options beyond ground beef, although you can find lean ground beef that has only 4 percent fat. Saturated fat is also found in cheap oil—like palm kernel oil—and junk foods that are made with these oils. Become a label reader—it can be eye opening. If something is high is trans fat or saturated fat, the nutritional value will be diminished. It's also common sense that any food fried in fat is going to be higher in calories and bad fat. There's a huge caloric/fat difference between fried chicken and charbroiled chicken, just as there's a big difference between a baked potato and a French fry.

Choose fruits and vegetables as often as possible—they are loaded with nutrients and anti-oxidants, therefore their health benefits are incredible. Bananas, strawberries, apples, oranges, grapefruits, tomatoes, green leafy vegetables, green peppers, red peppers, carrots, cabbage, green beans, peas, broccoli—each offers a variety of health benefits. Think about loading your plate with a rainbow of colors. Another great tip at the grocery store is to spend more time on the outer edges than in the middle. The outer edges are where you'll find whole, fresh foods—meats, eggs, dairy, whole grains, fruits, and veggies. The inner aisles contain more processed foods.

In your quest for good nutrition, always focus on the positives— what you should put into your diet—rather than what you should elim-inate. Great choices are whole grains (100 percent whole wheat products, brown rice, whole oats); low-fat foods that are high in mono and polysaturated fats; fruits and vegetables; and good oils (olive oil and even canola oil, as opposed to butter and animal fats). In addition, we all absolutely need a good supply of protein in our diets. I suggest one serv-ing with every meal. It builds new tissue and keeps you full. Choose something lean, such as chicken, fish, lean red meat, or eggs. The goal is to switch from ingesting empty calories that drive up our blood sugar and body fat to dense, nutritious foods.

Drink more water. Water hydrates the body and helps our digestive systems work better. Water even helps expedite the burning of body fat. Some drinks, such as caffeinated soft drinks, actually dehydrate you. I'm not saying that you should eliminate caffeine altogether, but don't let inferior beverages replace your water intake, because both alcohol and caffeine dehydrate the body. Fruit juice is fine, but not in large quantities, as most varieties have a lot of fructose and calories and do not hydrate as well as water. Always look for 100 percent juice, not a juice "drink" or "cocktail," since these beverages have little or no nutritional value.

TIPS FOR GOOD NUTRITION

We've all heard that breakfast is the most important meal of the day, and here's why: Breakfast means to *break* the *fast*. Let's say you've slept for eight hours, and you didn't eat anything for two hours before you went to bed. That means you've basically fasted for ten hours. When you don't eat, your metabolism slows down. When you break the fast, or eat breakfast, your metabolism gets stoked up again. It will also get your blood sugar up, send some energy to your brain and your muscles, and prevent you from feeling sluggish and headachy. If you skip breakfast, your blood sugar will continue to drop and your metabolism will stay sluggish, and you won't feel as energetic. Also, for those who skip breakfast there's a tendency to eat nothing but junk food for the rest of the day. I encourage the people that I work with to always have protein at breakfast—this can come from milk, eggs, or some other lean source of protein—whatever will satiate you.

Studies have shown that rather than having three large meals a day, it is healthier to have four to six smaller meals throughout the day. We call this "grazing." It's best to go no more than four hours during the day without eating, because after four hours the blood sugar begins to drop. When we don't eat regularly, we allow ourselves to become starved, causing us to overindulge with two gigantic meals and possibly a big sugary snack as well—the worst way to eat.

Enjoy your food! God gave us foods that are astoundingly varied with complex flavors, and if we're hungry we can appreciate them. But when we're eating to fill a hole in our soul, food will never ever satisfy, no matter how much we eat. This just might be the key to this entire book: Eat when you're hungry. That's it—pretty simple, right? Are you eating out of a true hunger and a need to be energized? Are you enjoying food the way it was meant to be enjoyed?

Activity can also help you eat better. When I go for a light hike, then maybe some strength training at the Y, and then a nice relaxing shower, I feel great about myself. And this great feeling almost always causes me to choose healthier food. I want to keep that great, healthy feeling! This is especially true if I'm spiritually and emotionally healthy as well. But if I don't exercise, and I'm stressed, or not at peace with relationships in my life, I eat poorly. I make poor choices, and reach for comfort food. That's also when I seem to have no sense of portion control; I just keep eating and eating. When eating is not about enjoying a meal or restoring energy, it's likely to send us into negative patterns of emotional eating and making poor food choices. What if, instead of eating when you felt lonely or depressed, you went for a walk or a bike ride, or some other activity you find enjoyable? You might discover new energy, a sense of well-being, and a deeper connection with God.

I recommend doing your cardio first thing in the morning, right before breakfast. If you wake up, drink a big glass of water, and go for a brisk walk, your body, which is in a fasted state, will efficiently call on stored fat for its energy. If you eat a big breakfast and then do cardio, your body will be use up the blood sugar from that breakfast, rather than burning stored fat. If first thing in the morning isn't your ideal time to exercise, wait a few hours after eating and do strength training before you do cardio. That way, your strength training will use up the blood sugar from your food (it's anaerobic activity—"without oxygen"), and then the aerobic activity, or cardio, will call on the stored body fat.

Losing weight is really a rather simple math problem. If you burn more calories than you take in, you'll lose weight. But you want to make certain you are losing body fat rather than water and muscle. It's essential to increase muscle mass and decrease body fat with a combination of cardio, strength training, good food, and *plenty* of water. The most important part of a healthy lifestyle is staying active. I'll say it again: *find an activity that you truly enjoy.* Find something that brings as much joy to your life as walking brings to mine.

Enjoy your relationship with food. Eating can be one of the most pleasurable experiences in life—God meant for it to be. But use common sense in your approach to food—make healthy choices and watch portion sizes. Drink six to eight glasses of water a day. Cut down on junk food—processed foods and sweets. When you do crave something sweet, try to make it reasonable and small. Find a way to have your favorites in moderation and really enjoy them.

Restrictive diets do not work. They are not the answer. The most important factor in living a healthy, robust life is becoming active. My hope is to inspire you to do simple things—to find an activity you love and that adds to your spiritual life, to make better food choices, and to learn to love your body as God created it.

REFLECTION QUESTIONS

What steps can you take today to change your perception of your body?

What steps can you take today to change your eating habits?

In this chapter, we discussed the difference between being healthy and being thin. If you were healthy, how would you be different? What does "healthy" mean to you?

How do you connect your spiritual life with your physical body?

How can becoming healthy help fulfill God's purpose for your life?

REFLECTIONS

REFLECTIONS

REFLECTIONS

.

MY PERSONAL PLAN OF CHANGE

SAMPLE PLAN OF CHANGE

Create a daily plan to allow God to give you relief from your image-related addictions—whether your addiction is the pursuit of physical perfection, or an addiction to food, or both. Begin the process by briefly describing vulnerable areas in your spirit, mind, and body. List and contact a dependable set of people to support you in what you are about to undertake. These people should be safe, supportive, visionary, encouraging, and they should be willing to keep you accountable. Write down the lies that you have believed about yourself and your body, and the specific habits that keep you in a cycle of unhealthy despair. Replace them with affirming truths about yourself. Describe the inner life you desire—without immediate physical changes. Begin by working on your mental and spiritual desires. Then list the changes you hope to see in your body image. List the steps you can take to begin this journey of balance and freedom from the bonds of image obsession and food addiction.

Read through the following sample Personal Plan of Change before completing your own plan.

Self Assessment: My name is Rachael, and I am thirty-seven years old. I have always had issues with my body. In middle school, I started noticing I was a little chubbier than my friends were. When I became teenager, I started dieting like crazy, but I could never stay on a diet for more than a few weeks. I also fasted and worked out for hours some days. But I got tired of trying. My weakness with food frustrated me, so I continued to gain weight throughout high school and college. When I got married, I thought it would change my eating habits. It didn't. By the time I had children, I was thirty to forty pounds overweight.

About five years ago, my husband and I stopped going to church regularly. Around the same time I lost my mother and started a new job. I've been hoping to feel okay about the way I look, but sometimes I feel hopeless. I feel like I'll never win the battle between dieting and accepting myself as I am.

Step One: List Your Issues

Spirit: I'm disconnected from God. I'm angry with Him because He gave me this body.

Mind: I'm depressed about what I see in the mirror and how others must see me. I'm embarrassed when I have to show up in public in a swimsuit or shorts. I can't stop thinking about food or my terrible body image. I can't stand the way I look, and I don't know if I've ever liked the way I look. I wonder what my husband really thinks.

Body: I've never liked my body. I was pudgy as a child, and then I gained more and more weight as an adult. Having kids hasn't helped. I never stay with an exercise program, and I feel intimidated to work out around others. I feel inadequate, but I can't stop eating.

Step Two: Goals

Spirit: I will reconnect with God, and allow Him to heal my relationship with Him and my dissatisfaction with my body. I want peace and happiness, the gift of life.

Mind: I want to be free from my mental obsession with food and my body. I want to wake up in the morning and have a positive anticipation about my day, instead of waking up depressed about my negative experience with food and my body. I want to look forward to my interactions with people, and become free of my addiction to food.

Body: I will become physically active on a daily basis. I look forward to exercising and enjoying a new lifestyle that is active and peaceful. I will reduce my body fat as a byproduct of my new active and healthy lifestyle. I will eat when I am hungry and stop when I am full. I want energy.

Step Three: Support Groups and Individuals

Support Community:

women's small group at church, twelve-step program

Individual Support:

Suzie (church mentor)

Gretchen (long time close friend and supporter)

Pastor McMillan,

Grace (accountability partner)

Step Four: Your Vision

I will stop my daily obsession with food and how I look. My life will not be controlled by these constant thoughts, which will free me to become physically active for the health benefits. I'll eat when I'm hungry, and I'll enjoy food. I'll no longer eat to stuff feelings or comfort inner pain, and I'll be fulfilled by God. I'll be a happier person, filled with a permanent joy that is not based on how I'm looking or eating. I'll be free to serve my Lord and be a tool in His service. I'll have a renewed passion and energy for living that I do not have right now.

Step Five: Your Prayer

Lord, I know that I have put my trust in myself for too long. I know now that I can't conquer my addictions without You to pull me through. I am not strong enough to pull myself out of my cycles of compulsion and obsession. I cannot see myself the way You see me without Your help. I cannot love my family the way I should without Your freedom, handed to me when I have no strength to even take it. I understand that it will take diligence and seeking after You. I ask that You never stop completing the good work You have begun in me. I ask for healing, and I trust that You will provide it. Amen.

CREATING YOUR PERSONAL PLAN OF CHANGE

Self-Assessment: Write a paragraph describing your journey so far and your relationship with food, body, God, self, and others. What thoughts have you had about your body for most of your life? What do you think about your body now? How often do you think about it? What was your relationship with food like as you were growing up? What is your relationship with food now?

Step One: Listing Your Issues

Spirit (for example, anger toward God, blame, despair, disconnection)

Mind (for example, self-loathing, bitterness toward others, obsessions)

Body (for example, diets, unhealthy lifestyle, cycle of habit, eating disorders)

Step Two: Goals

Write individual goals for each issue you have struggled with, and list specific steps you will take with God's help.

Spirit

Mind

Body

Step Three: Support Groups and Individuals

Find a support community. Below are resources that can help you in this quest.

Restore Ministries (www.restoreymca.org)
Overeaters Anonymous (www.oa.org)
Other:

Find individuals to support you. List at least one individual in each category below who will support you and share your journey to recovery.

Friend:
Sponsor:
Therapist:
Counselor:
Doctor:

Pastor:

Life Coach:

Personal Trainer:

Nutritionist:

Physical Therapist:

Other:

Step Four: Your Vision

Write a description of what your life will be like when you are well on the road to recovery. Explain how you will be able to live your life to the fullest.

Step Five: Your Prayer

A faith-based life is one of complete and total powerlessness over every compulsion. Only God can give you the freedom you seek. Write a prayer that you can repeat every day while you are working through this liberation from the body-related struggles that bind you.

CONCLUSION

Making peace with our bodies, learning to love who we are from the inside out, is critical if we are going to enjoy our lives. We only get one life, one body. We don't get to turn it in and order a new one. Learning to be comfortable with our bodies is paramount to enjoying life.

I was just talking with a seventy-year-old man who comes to the YMCA every day on his lunch hour. He talked of the great joy that he has received from being active. I hope that you have learned from this study that you can have a positive relationship with your body and with food. God bless you, my friend, as He leads you on your journey to hope, health, and happiness.

TIPS FOR LEADING A JOURNEY TO FREEDOM SMALL GROUP

Welcome and thank you for accepting the challenge of leading others along their own journeys to freedom. These tips are designed to aid you in creating a small group setting that is productive and full of hope, health, and happiness.

PREPARATION

Being well prepared will help alleviate any anxiety you may have about leading your group. When you know what you want to accomplish in your group, it will help you stay on track with the lesson plan. Plus, if you're not prepared, participants will pick up on your lack of preparation, which might affect their own dedication to the group and the process of change. In extreme cases, lack of preparation may even cause you to lose some participants. If the leader is not committed, why should the participants be committed? So come to your group prepared to lead them.

Be a role model. A good facilitator is simply a model group participant. Be on time. Be prepared. Do your homework. Guard against moodiness.

Be consistent. Be positive. Be a good listener. Maintain confidentiality. Be enthusiastic.

Recognize your limitations. It is important that you remember that you are not responsible for the results of your group. You are not responsible to "fix" anyone. You are not a counselor, a therapist, or a minister. You are a mentor, one who is helping guide another down a path that you have traveled before. Each participant is responsible for his or her own life and journey.

OPENING THE GROUP SESSION

Use gentleness and patience as you pace the progress of the group. Rushing through the lessons might be exhausting for your participants. Try to find some kind of meaningful devotional, excerpt from a book, or song to emphasize and complement what you are studying for the week.

Plan your time so that you are able to get through the majority of the recommended questions in each less on, but more important, be prepared to settle for quality of questions and answers over quantity. The goal is to have a productive meeting. Getting through every question in the lesson may seem optimal, but it may not accomplish the goal.

BE AWARE

Avoid being the center of attention during group time. Your role as leader is to get the group involved in sharing, to keep the discussion moving forward and on topic, and to make sure that your group is on time and the necessary material is covered. You are there to give direction and guidance to the group, but avoid dominating the group by talking too much in the sessions.

Be aware of your group dynamics. As a facilitator, get to know your group members. In order to help them as much as possible, you need to be aware and in tune with their needs. Pay attention to the members' body language, their actions, and what they are saying and sharing. Assess the participants in their response and in their openness (or lack of).

Don't let any one member dominate the group. Handling the "talker" in your group will require some skill. Be careful, because if one member begins to dominate your group, it can alienate some of the more reserved members. If one member is opening up and sharing for long periods of time, try not to let this member's problems control the group. Say, "I would love to continue this discussion with you after the meeting. Will that be okay?" This will keep you from appearing uncaring and will give the group permission to get back on track. Also, think about positioning. Sit beside these individuals instead of across from them to avoid prolonged eye contact. When presenting a question or topic for discussion, put a time limit on responses. If someone runs over the limit, don't be afraid to break in and praise the person's point, but then raise a new question back to the group about what was shared. Validate the individual's feelings and input, but then focus the discussion.

Allow silence. Often, facilitators become uncomfortable with silence in group discussions. Sometimes it is good to have a moment of silence so that the participants will speak up and start owning the conversation. Do not feel like you have to fill the void. If the group members think you are going to fill the silence, then they will learn to wait for you. If you find that there has been a considerable amount of time given to answer a question and no one is speaking up, you might ask them why they are silent or move on to another question.

Contain the desire to rescue. If someone gets emotionally upset or begins to cry and show emotion during the session, avoid anything that could interfere with the member feeling the emotion of the moment. Let the individual express the emotions and deal with them, even if they are painful. While the person is sharing, do not reach over and hug, touch, or comfort. After the individual has finished sharing and is done, then offer a hug if you desire or thank and affirm the person for speaking courageously.

Use self-disclosure appropriately. One element of being a good facilitator is a willingness to be vulnerable and to share your journey of change at the appropriate times. However, be careful that you do not use the group to deal with your unresolved issues.

As you lead discussion, consistently state and reiterate the boundaries of group discussion—confidentiality about what is spoken in the group, respect for each other, and the right to pass if a member doesn't feel comfortable sharing at the time. Accept what each person has to say without making sudden judgments. Be the primary catalyst in providing a warm, open, trusting, and caring atmosphere. This will help the group gradually take ownership.

CLOSING THE GROUP

Manage your time wisely. It is important that your group start and end on time. Strive for consistency, beginning with the first meeting by starting and ending on time and continuing that schedule each week.

SESSION ONE—INTRODUCTION WEEK

Lesson Goal:

In your first meeting you will not cover any material. You will begin to get to know each other as a group and learn the structure and guidelines for the next eight weeks, as well as the expectations of each participant.

Leading the Session:

Welcome the participants and commend them on taking this action to pursue change in their lives.

Ask each participant to share whatever information they are

comfortable sharing about themselves with the group: name, occupation, number and ages of children and or grandchildren, where you were born, how you heard of this group, etc. are good places to start. Be sure that you and your co-facilitator (if applicable) introduce yourselves first to increase the group's comfort level.

Show the first session of Scott Reall's video (if applicable), talk about what they have to look forward to as a group in the upcoming eight weeks, and present group guidelines to the participants:

Confidentiality is of the utmost importance.

Group members are not required to talk but encouraged to do so.

Agree to accept each other and to encourage one another.

We do not give advice, or try to "fix" or rescue other group members.

Be honest.

Be on time.

Agree to make the weekly meetings and the daily work a priority.

Ask if anyone would like to ask a question or add a group guideline. The goal is for participants to feel safe, secure and encouraged.

Choose one of the following warm-up questions to open up the group and begin to break the ice:

What do you like to do when you have free time?

What brings you great joy?

What is a special talent or skill that you possess?

Pair your group into couples, and give each person five minutes to answer the following questions to each other:

What brought you here today?

What in your life do you want to change?

What excuses will you give yourself to not come to group or do your homework?

Closing the Group

Encourage the group members to come back to the next meeting.

Encourage group members to read and answer the questions at the end of the chapter to be discussed next week and to write their answers in the blank space provided. Tell them to come next week ready to discuss.

Assign accountability partners for each participant and, if possible, pair them with the partner that they were paired with for the last exercise. Ask them to exchange phone numbers and e-mail addresses.

Accountability Partner Guidelines:

Discuss the specifics of the change each person is trying to achieve.

Relate how each person is doing in spirit, mind, and body.

Ask your partner about his or her struggles, problems, and particular difficulties.

Be considerate of each other's time and situations, and remember that the purpose is to discuss change.

Make an effort to take the conversation beyond a superficial level.

The Importance of Accountability Partners:

One of the best tools to help us through the rough times in our journey to freedom is accountability. Often we don't realize how much accountability has influenced and affected our decisions throughout our lives. We are accountable to get to work on time or we may lose our jobs. In school, athletes have to keep their grades up, attend class, and get to practice or they are off the team. In the same way, unless we have some sort of accountability, many of us will not sustain our efforts to change. We need accountability to develop the discipline of sticking with something, especially if consistency is hard for us.

Be sure and thank them for coming this week. Express how excited you are to be with them and to discover where this journey is going to take all of you as a group.

Close with prayer, singing, saying the serenity prayer, or any positive way you feel appropriate.

SESSIONS 2 THROUGH 7—COVERING THE STUDY GUIDE MATERIAL

For these six weeks, you will be covering Chapters 1 through 6 in the study guide. You will want to follow and review the guidelines for preparing for leading a small group. Once each session begins thank everyone for being there and then begin to go over that week's readings and have members share about what stood out to them in the lesson. You will then want to go over the questions at the end of the chapter for the rest of your time. If some do not want to share their answers, do not force them. Thank everyone that shares for participating and encourage those that don't. Encourage members to use the Reflection pages at he end of each chapter during the week for journaling and notes. End in prayer.

SESSION 8—CREATING PERSONAL PLANS OF CHANGE

Leading the Session:

Go over the group guidelines for respecting participants as they share their plans.

Have participants read action plans aloud.

Have them sign the places provided in their books, committing them to follow the plans of action they have created.

Talk about the specific next steps that they can take (for example, enrolling in a twelve-steps or other recovery program or a personal training or exercise program).

Make sure they have all the resources they need to fulfill their action plans.

Thank them for coming and close in prayer.

Hold hands and sing "Amazing Grace."

NOTES

Chapter One

1. Carlin Flora, "The Beguiling Truth About Beauty," *Psychology Today* Magazine, May/Jun 2006, 22.
2. Jill Neimark, "The Beefcaking of America," *Psychology Today* Magazine, Nov/Dec 1994, http://www.psychologytoday.com/articles/index.php?term=pto-19941101-000021.xml.
3. National Eating Disorders Association, "Statistics: Eating Disorders and Their Precursors," 2002, http://www.niu.edu/csdc/STATS.pdf.
4. *Reader's Digest*, October 1991, 62.
5. National Eating Disorders Association, "Statistics: Eating Disorders and Their Precursors," 2002, http://www.niu.edu/csdc/STATS.pdf.
6. "Archive: Sympathy by Paul Laurence Dunbar," Poetry Foundation, http://www.poetryfoundation.org/archive/poem.html?id=175756.
7. Romans 7:16

Chapter Two

1. James O. Prochaska, John Norcross, and Carlo DiClemente, *Changing for Good* (New York: Collins, 2007), 48.
2. Mark 10:27

Chapter Three

1. *Random House Webster's College Dictionary*, s.v. "affirmation."
2. Roseanne Olson, "Body Images," *More* Magazine, April 2007.
3. Charles Swindoll, *The Tale of the Tardy Oxcart* (Nashville: W Publishing, 1998), 400.

Chapter Four

1. Jan Bono, "A Burden to Share," Guideposts, March 2003.
2. Ibid.
3. Ibid.
4. Ibid.
5. Ibid.

Chapter Five

1. Julia Cameron, *The Artist's Way* (New York: Tarcher, 2002), 153.
2. Sally Squires, "A Fitness Icon Keeps His Juices Flowing," The Washington Post.com, June 12, 2007, http://www.washingtonpost.com/wp-dyn/content/article/2007/06/11/AR2007061101919_pf.html.
3. "Walking Away Depression," ThirdAge, Inc., http://www.thirdage.com/news/archive/ALT02991029-02.html.
4. "Integrate Exercise Into Your Life," Bodies by Hoffman, http://www.bodiesbyhoffman.com/news.html.

5. "The Real Reason You Regain Weight," The Body Fat Guide, http://www.bodyfatguide.com/regainweight.html.

Chapter Six

1. "George Bernard Shaw Quotes," BrainyMedia.com, http://www.brainyquote.com/quotes/quotes/g/georgebern131494.html.